LITTLE LIBRARY NUMBER FIVE

MARY ROBINSON

JOHN & FATTI BURKE

GILL BOOKS

Mary Bourke was born in Ballina, County Mayo, in 1944. She was a brilliant student and always worked hard. Even though both of her parents were doctors, Mary wanted to study law.

UNIVERSITAS DUBLINIENSIS

mary Bourke

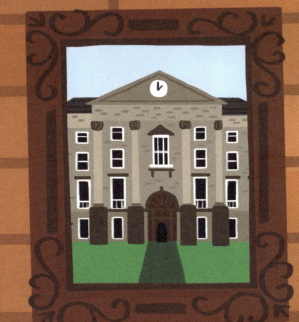

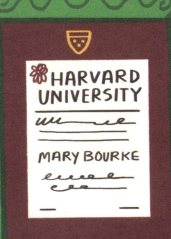

HARVARD UNIVERSITY

MARY BOURKE

After secondary school, she went to Trinity College Dublin and then on to Harvard in America. She joked that having four brothers gave her an interest in women's rights.

At the age of 25, Mary became the youngest professor of law in Ireland.

She wanted to use her skills and passion to make the world a better place, not only for women, but also for the poor and underprivileged.

She was also the youngest person ever to be elected to Seanad Éireann, the upper house of the government, in 1969.

The Irish Times

"Equal Rights For All"

As a senator, Mary constantly campaigned for equal rights for women, the Traveller Community and the disadvantaged.

At that time, women didn't have to sit on juries and very few were asked to. Women who worked in the civil service also had to give up their jobs if they got married! But Mary changed all that.

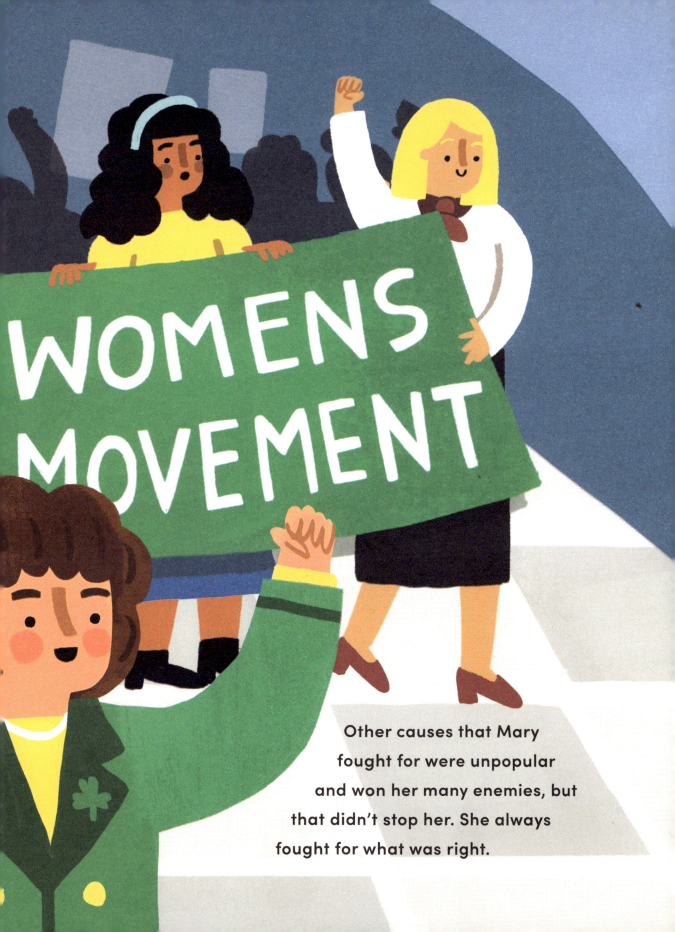

WOMENS MOVEMENT

Other causes that Mary fought for were unpopular and won her many enemies, but that didn't stop her. She always fought for what was right.

When Dublin Corporation wanted to build new offices on an old Viking settlement, Mary and thousands of others protested. They didn't want the Viking settlement to be destroyed.

Mary and the protesters fought hard, but this was a battle they didn't win and the offices were built at Wood Quay in Dublin.

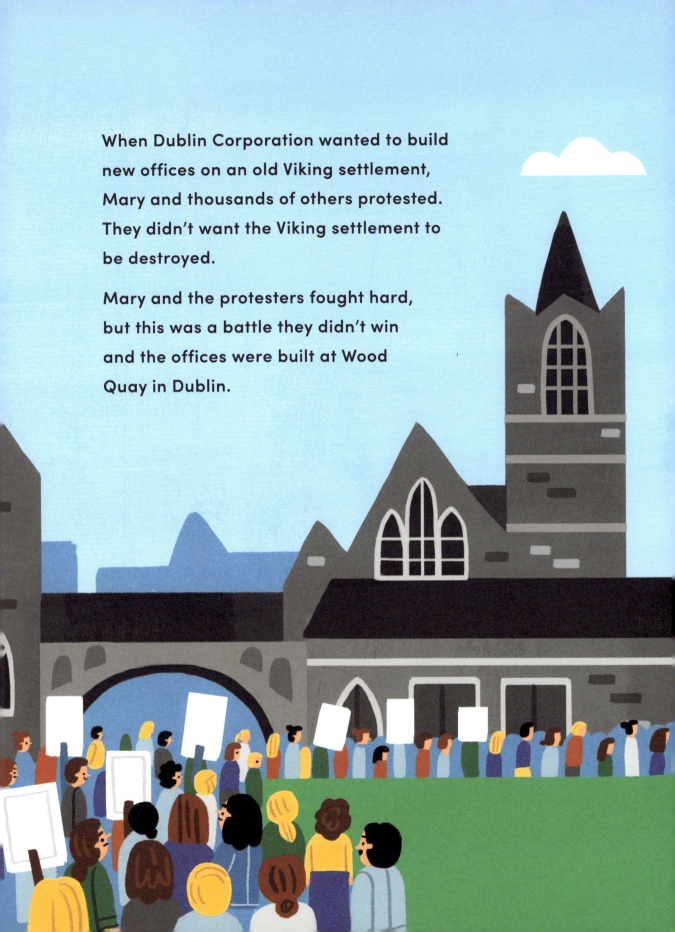

VOTE Nº 1

MARY ROBINSON

A President with a purpose

Mary was asked to run for the presidency in 1990 when President Patrick Hillery retired. Some people said that it was no job for a woman, but this only made Mary more determined.

After a hard campaign, Mary made history by becoming the first female President of Ireland! She said, 'I was elected by the women of Ireland, who instead of rocking the cradle, rocked the system.'

President Robinson became very popular when she visited the people of Northern Ireland during the Troubles. She was warned not to go, but Mary was used to breaking new ground and the people liked her for it.

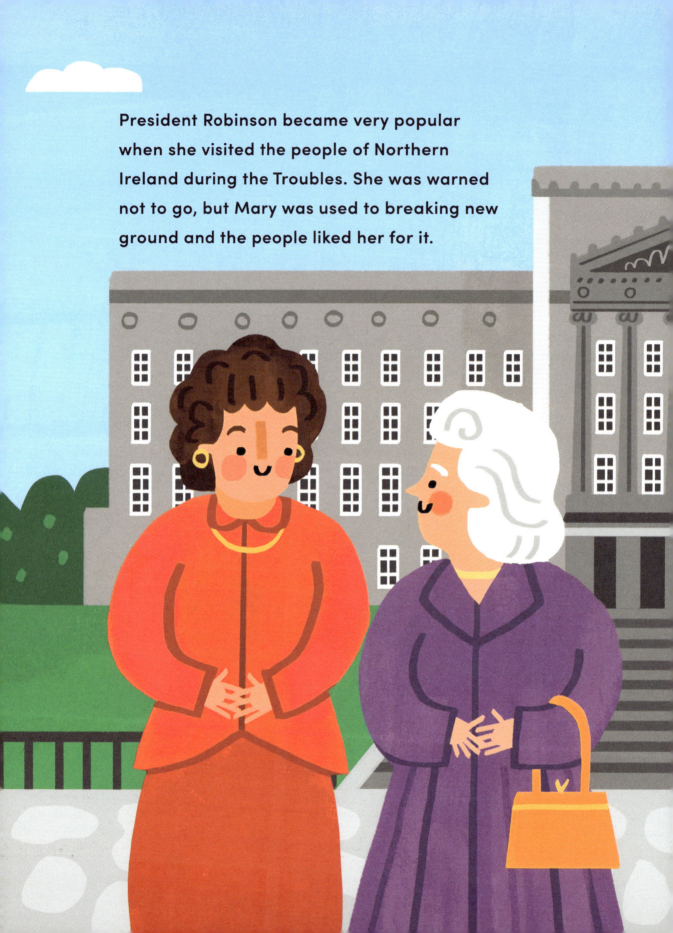

As President, she reached out not just to the whole of Ireland, but to many other countries around the world.

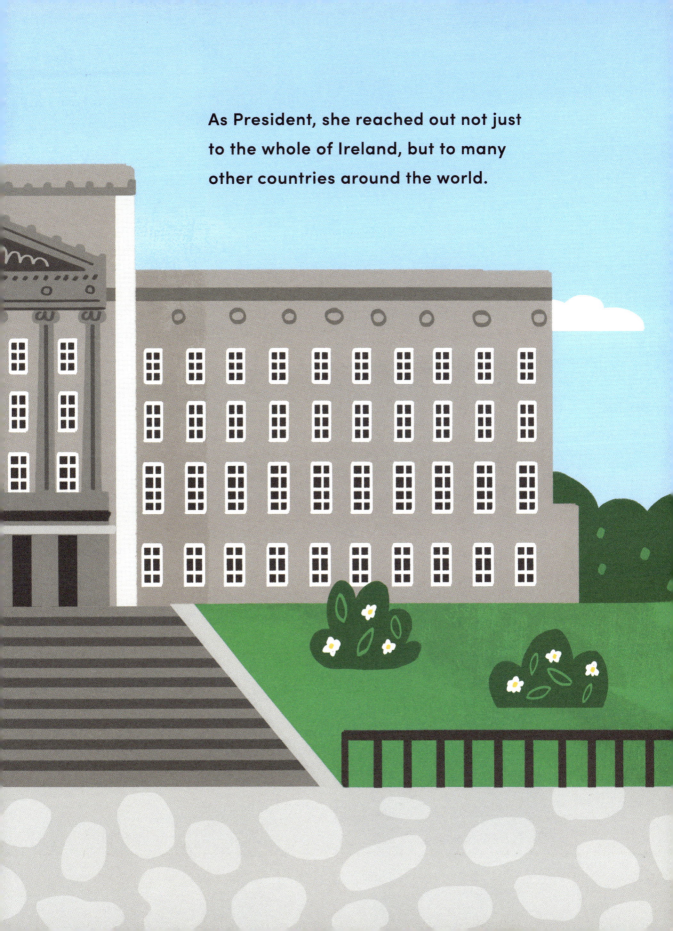

President Robinson was the first head of state to visit Somalia after its civil war and famine. She also visited Rwanda and drew the world's attention to the suffering there.

She was very upset by the poverty and hunger that she saw in these and many other countries.

Mary decided she could do even more good by joining the United Nations as High Commissioner for Human Rights, so she resigned as President of Ireland in 1997 to start her new job.

She was now Commissioner Robinson and she paid
special attention to children's issues such as the need
for food, clean water, shelter and healthcare. Her
work took her all over the world, particularly to Africa.

Mary cares deeply about the environment. She thinks climate change is the most important issue facing humanity.

She says that we should make climate change personal in our lives by doing whatever we can to help, like recycling and using less water.

Mary doesn't eat meat and tries to only use public transport.

Reduce
Reuse
Recycle

Mary set up The Mary Robinson Foundation –
Climate Justice to help those who are most affected
by climate change: the poorest and most vulnerable
people in the world.

In her work with the foundation, Mary has brought her
passion for human rights and climate change together.

Mary has received many awards. US President Barack Obama presented her with the Medal of Freedom. He said, 'She speaks up for the hungry and the hunted, the forgotten and the ignored. She is showing the way to a better future for the world.'

Mary continues to
be a voice for justice
and fairness.

Timeline

1944
Mary is born in Ballina on 21 May

1963
Wins scholarship to Trinity College Dublin

1969
Becomes a member of the Seanad

1967
Mary is called to the Irish Bar

1970
Marries Nicholas Robinson

1979
Elected to Dublin Corporation

1980
Called to the Inner Bar as Senior Council

1998

Becomes Chancellor of
Trinity College

2007

Mary becomes a
member of The Elders, a
group founded by Nelson
Mandela

1997

Mary becomes United
Nations High Commissioner
for Human Rights

2010

The Mary Robinson
Foundation – Climate
Justice is formed

1990

Elected President of
Ireland 1990–1997

2014

Mary becomes UN
Special Envoy on
Climate Change

1988

Mary and her husband
Nick found the Irish Centre
for European Law in Trinity

2018

Appointed Chair
of The Elders

Did You Know?

Mary Robinson has received over **15 AWARDS** from around the world, including the **ERASMUS PRIZE**, **INDIRA GHANDI PRIZE**, **THE OTTO HAHN PEACE MEDAL** in Gold of the UN Association of Germany, and the **SYDNEY PEACE PRIZE**.

In the 1980s, Mary was elected to the **INTERNATIONAL COMMISSION OF JURISTS** in **GENEVA**.

When she was elected **CHANCELLOR** of **TRINITY COLLEGE** in 1998, she was the first woman to fill the post.

In 1970, she married **NICHOLAS ROBINSON**, a solicitor, historian and cartoonist. They have **THREE CHILDREN**.

At **CHRISTMAS TIME**, Mary followed the **OLD IRISH CUSTOM** of having a **LIGHT SHINING IN THE WINDOW** as a welcome to all Irish people throughout the world.

When Mary ran for the **PRESIDENCY**, she was nominated by the **LABOUR PARTY** and supported by the **GREEN PARTY** and the **WORKERS' PARTY**.

Mary was the **FIRST IRISH PRESIDENT** to **VISIT** the **UNITED KINGDOM** and **MEET QUEEN ELIZABETH II**.

In 2007, NELSON MANDELA announced the formation of a new group called THE ELDERS. This is a group of world leaders who contribute their WISDOM, INDEPENDENT LEADERSHIP and HONESTY to tackle some of the WORLD'S TOUGHEST PROBLEMS. The group also included Graça Machel, Kofi Annan, Ela Bhatt, Gro Harlem Brundtland, former US President Jimmy Carter, Li Zhaoxing and Muhammad Yunus. In 2018, Mary became CHAIR OF THE ELDERS.

In 2001, Mary served as SECRETARY GENERAL of the WORLD CONFERENCE against RACISM, RACIAL DISCRIMINATION, XENOPHOBIA and related INTOLERANCE which was held in SOUTH AFRICA.

BOOKS by Mary Robinson include *Climate Justice*, *Everybody Matters*, *A Voice for Human Rights* and *A Voice for Somalia*.

ABOUT the AUTHORS

KATHI 'FATTI' BURKE is an illustrator from County Waterford.

JOHN BURKE is Fatti's dad. He is a retired primary school teacher and principal. He lives in Waterford.

Their first book, *Irelandopedia*, won The Ryan Tubridy Show Listeners' Choice Award at the Irish Book Awards 2015, and the Eilís Dillon Award for first children's book and the Judges' Special Award at the CBI Book of the Year Awards 2016. Their next books, *Historopedia* and *Foclóiropedia*, were nominated for the Specsavers Children's Book of the Year (Junior) Award at the Irish Book Awards 2016 and 2017. Their books have sold over 100,000 copies in Ireland.

ALSO in the LITTLE LIBRARY SERIES

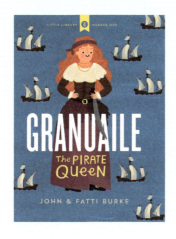

BOOK ONE

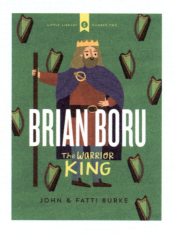

BOOK TWO

BOOK THREE

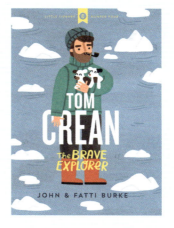

BOOK FOUR

Gill Books
Hume Avenue
Park West
Dublin 12
www.gillbooks.ie

Gill Books is an imprint of M.H. Gill and Co.

Text © John Burke 2020
Illustrations © Kathi Burke 2020
978 07171 8993 9

Designed by www.grahamthew.com
Printed by Hussar Books, Poland

This book is typeset in 13pt on 25pt Sofia Pro

The paper used in this book comes from the wood pulp of
managed forests. For every tree felled, at least one tree is
planted, thereby renewing natural resources.

A CIP catalogue record for this book is available from the British
Library.

5 4 3 2 1